Abder-Rahmane Derradji

NOSTALGIA

Abder-Rahmane Derradji

NOSTALGIA

Nostalgia

JustFiction Edition

Imprint

Any brand names and product names mentioned in this book are subject to trademark, brand or patent protection and are trademarks or registered trademarks of their respective holders. The use of brand names, product names, common names, trade names, product descriptions etc. even without a particular marking in this work is in no way to be construed to mean that such names may be regarded as unrestricted in respect of trademark and brand protection legislation and could thus be used by anyone.

Cover image: www.ingimage.com

Publisher:
JustFiction! Edition
is a trademark of
Dodo Books Indian Ocean Ltd., member of the OmniScriptum S.R.L Publishing group
str. A.Russo 15, of. 61, Chisinau-2068, Republic of Moldova Europe
Printed at: see last page
ISBN: 978-620-3-57876-8

NOSTALGIA

DEDICATION

This work goes for Poetry lovers

Table of Contents

I Do Not Know How To Impress An Empress

I am in a mess,
My life is in a mess,
 I have no skills, no romance to give,
And much less,
Less than you expect dear,
Don't be in fear,
And don't stare at me like if I came from
Alcatraz,

How to impress the empress?
And you are here still standing
For me to give you a nice word,
A poem,
Covered in a dress,
A dress of feelings, emotions,
Smooth touches,
Well organised like a chess

I told you that I am an army soldier,
Who knows nothing about love,
Or feelings, I am designed
To kill
To kill everything that moves around you,
And around me
And I don't care less,
Sorry they made me that way
They trained me to hate,
To beat, to torture, to beat the hell of you all
And to harass,

Sorry dear,
They made me that way
And I don't know how to humanise me
And be like you all to feel,
To talk the talk, and do the walk you do all
And love tenderly
And cry like a baby
And when I am hurt,
And stop my beloved caresses me
And my shoulders,

Then breathes inside my ear
Air of love,
Air of tenderness and much more
Oh dear that's what I love
And that's what I wish for
But right now I am done and my time is due,
Captain! I am coming,
Yes sir, Yes sir!
Bye my empress!

Looking For My Palestina

I Came To the Medina
Looking for my Palestina
Baby my Baby
Where are you?
Still under the rubbles?
Still alive my Diva
Oh my Devina!

The Highways robbers,
The snitch, the pimps of the Dollar,
And of the Shekel,
Still abusing the little
Ballerina,

But she defied them all,
And she is still standing on one little toe,
With no support,
Since she became,
Now lonely in an orphelinat
My beloved, my adorable
Palestina!

Live, and live and live now,
And in the future,
Despite the A...Rabs
And the Gulf lackeys
And Al Alkami of the Palace,
Still serving his bosses,
In the Medina,

Snitching, selling his own meat,
His own flesh and honour to the Zombies,
Who used Red Indians,
Puerto Ricans,
And poor destitute,
Oppressed Latina

But remember my hero,
Who reduced those to zero,
That was once, in the famous,
Battle of all battles,
Of Hattina!

Saladin here he lives today,
And tomorrow,
With a million and a billion,
Enforced by men of deed,
Not of a creed,
And true soldiers,
Martyrs, Mudjahideena!

Everyone Is A Novel Darling

Everyone is a novel, and I love to read it,
So show me the chapters of your inner heart,
I would not bother much about the title,
But I promise that I would read it,
From cover to cover,
I promise that I would read it attentively,
With passion, and tenderness,
Because I love books, I love souls,
Human souls!
I love all what it's all about,
And promise that I will not reveal its secrets, and its bad vices if any,
So just show me your heart,
Your soul, your inner book,
Your story with all its good and bad,
Fame, failure, and Glory!
Man! I am impatient to wait!

Miss You Can Wait

Miss, you can wait!
He came in,
Then never came out,
I think,
I believe in a few minutes,
It would be over, and he would be out
Thirty minutes passed,
An hour
Two three, then he would be free,
God! It took longer,
But now I think,
I believe

I can stress it now,
That he would never be out,
And it's time to loud my voice and shout!
Khashoooggi! Come out!
No voice no screams,
No response, no nothing,
But dead total silence,
And only the whistling wind,
And the flying vultures,
And the human hungry hyenas,
And the assassins just consumed his body,
Devoured him alive,

And the rest just melted away in the air
With no trace, no prints
No nothing, no blood stains,
It's all a drought,
Whom do I blame?
The Istanbul Khalifa,
Or the mighty Sultan with his eighteen Dober-men
Or himself that he went in,
In the first place?
But now I doubt,
He would never return,

But think that there are hundreds of you,
Thousands like you who did not have a chance,
Like you did, to be heard,
And to be celebrated,
In style and what a style!

Al Quds The Eternal Capital Of Palestine

Loud your voice high,
And repeat after me,
Al Quds! Jerusalem!
Nay Urshalim,
It's free but not for sale or hire!

Al Quds, capital of all Palestine
From north to south,
From east to west,
The eternal city, the mighty city,
The whole and the empire,

Trump, turns tramp,
And the shithole of countries,
That he despised, hated,
But forgot his native German village,
The 'Mire'!

He displayed the entire white house,
The mighty house,
Furniture and co for sale
But failed to find a buyer,

But sooner or later,
Will be confused
Or what the US is made of,
Nations, peoples, cultures
Of the empire,

Sooner or later Mr. Trump,
Or rather tramp,
If he still misbehaves,
And sets his own house,
The American peoples' house
On fire!

We do not know whether,
He is deranged, or an imposter,
We do not know if he's really,

Tracked a deal with Mr Nat,
And with the mobs
And with the high way robbers,
And with a Zionist,
The slayer,

To sell what does not belong to him,
We do not know either about his wish,
About his fish and dish,
Or was it simply part of his wicked
Desire?

But we swore that Al Quds,
The US, and with all its lovable people,
The whole country,
And the entire,

Know nothing of the plot
That gathered Mr Nat. And co,
And with a cheap Arabian Sheikh,
 That went under the table,
And on a secret parchment and
A flayer,

Oh! Believers,
Be patient now and wait,
For your saviour,
The coming Mahdi,
And for the truth and for the challenge,
And for the wicked and the false prophet,
To come and be defeated,
And for the imposter liar!

Make Revolution Not Love

Get a gun!
Get anything you could grab,
Get a feather, get a pen,
And a parchment,
Oh! Beauty dove,
And start revolting in your own way,
Your pen is an ICBM,
More powerful than the US's
And the North Koreans'
The nuts!!
Propaganda and mind-control,
Information,
Globalisation, bullying,
Corporations, multi-nationals,
Multi-what ****??
Slavery, a human for a dollar,
A woman for a cent, for a minute,
Babies for sale, refugees,
Refugitives
Just greed! Greed and more greed!
More hungry mouths,
Not enough to feed,
We need change,
We need a U turn,
But when you only turn,
With no return,
Back to nature,
Back to simplicity,
Back to my written letter,
Scrub this bloody email and delete it,
Let's be together,
And be one simple soul,
Then we may be able to see this change.

Post Brexit

Hex it or Brexit,
Now it's late to fix it
My God what have I done?
I slipped my polling card by mistake
And voted Brexit,
And here I am now at the crossroads
I messed it
Is it possible to reverse and right the wrong?
And fix it?
Or it's late for me after my lexit?
I jumped in the air with the hope to land safely
But here I am still floating in the sky
And I still do not know when, where and how I'll land
I messed it.
It serves me now to suffer and grief
And accept my fate and destiny,
After I minced it.

The Orlando Massacre And Afghan Tragedy

The policy of hate and date,
You may not like but it's the truth,
The bitter truth mate!
Was it a lone wolf terror or was it a coordinated fight?

Who cares since it targeted souls
Despised by night.
But you are no God to legislate and
Decide on fate

An act that made an end,
To the destiny of a foe and a friend...
With no reason,
In a season of hate and revenge?

In Orlando like in Kabul,
A score of lives fell like flies,
With no respect to the being and soul,
Not to dare to compare the two,
You lunatic! You fool!

In Orlando like in Kabul, human tokens
From all sort of life dropped and stopped
Thinking, stopped moving and stopped breathing,
For some sick and dick, this was cool????
For others, this was a life crime!

But the difference, is that in Orlando unlike in Kabul,
Media and support were promptly presented and shoulders were
Provided to lean and cry upon,
But in Kabul you are on your own but not alone,
Blood called blood and this is a twin evil
To face and confront,

I know that all of us are divided and different,
I know for sure that our shaky unity in diversity is now compromised,
But human life is worth than principles of freedom and democracy if any
For sure God created Adam and eve,
Nay Adam and Steve,

But who cares now in this mega mall of globalised world
And as the oriental dictum goes, each sheep is hanged by its leg
And on its own,
And now you have all your time to grief cry and moan,
With your clan and tribe and even on your own,
Your acts reflect your thought,
Or maybe your act translates you hate,
Reflects you vision, your own vision,
That is your mission,

Terror calls terror and an eye for an eye is still on,
Reflecting an old Judaeo-Christian, then a Muslim law,
To celebrate hate at dawn

It's your shared [Onus!]
Your shared fault,
And now you are harvesting together,
It's now you shared a bonus,
Some of you still on the divine ship
Some of you still worshiping in deep,
You name Torah, Psalms, Bible and the Quran,
But some of you are still faithful to the [Cronus!]

The British June Referendum

Referenda! Referendum!
The big ban will make it boom!
Hopefully on June 23rd,
Listen to what I have just heard
Calls of: that is it! That's it!
It is time to jump,
It's time to Brexit

The beauty of Britain
Is in its uniqueness,
In its unity in diversity, in its commonwealth,
In its borrowed Kenyan tea,
In its Indian curry
In its jerk spicy Jamaican chicken and Chinese take-away,
In its Irish coffee and flavour,
And fish chips,
Which the empire,
Once upon a time mixed it

That's it! That's it!
It is time to close the gates,
Or maybe it's time to Brexit
Whether it will fit or not,
The opportunity is now here
To fix it.
Once and for all,
To decide and call the call
And play a role, its own role
And hex it.

Hex the bunch of Brussels
And the commission,
With the fake mission,
That intends to flex it

The union, the mighty union will soon
Crack down, if a Brexit, Greexit and the rest
Will definitely follow suit to lax it
But all this may not occur

And Britain will be doomed to remain
Imprisoned and blur,
For another century to come
And be a dictum for others to lance it.

Silence In The Age Of Omerta

I know what you know,
What he knows,
Whom he who killed,
But kept silent and blind,
I know what you know,
Who he muddled,
Who he murdered,
And dirtied the field,
I know what you know,
Who you slaughtered the soul,
Neither me, nor thee
Nay the remaining foul.
No hear, no see,
The law of Omerta is surely risky,
And dangerous,
He who does not now know,
But knows better than himself and you,
Who slaughtered the lad, bribed and fed,
Threatened and said,
No hear, no see,
Then smashed the calves in a bloody pool,
This evil monster, a son of a ghoul!
I have seen nothing, nor heard a thing,
Omerta is the rule and motto to survive now.

The Witch Curse

I curse you and thee,
I curse you north and south,
I curse you in stomach and mouth,
I curse you west and east,
I curse you body, shoulders and feet,
I curse you left and right,
I curse you in your hearing and sight,
I curse you in walking and running,
I curse you asleep and awake,
I curse you in real and fake,
I curse you until nothing is left of you,
Who does evil, harvest evil,
And you will be devoured by the devil,
By day and night,
Until you'll become weaker to fight,
Until you'll confuse the wrong from the right.

The Rose Refuses To Discharge Its Scent This Year

Petals closed,
Pale colour,
Bending leaves,
Bound roots,
This season is not like others,
The drought, the cracking earth,
The war, the calamity,
Had all contributed to its sadness,
Others are even worse,
Pele-mêle,
Here and there,
Lying on the ground,
As though they had aggressively been,
De-rooted, cut off from their earthly warmth,
And suddenly an unexpected storm,
Poured from the sky, lightning,
A bolt of thunder and,
Torrent of rains,
Then back again, to life,
Petals invitingly open themselves,
Leaves standing up like a hound, vigilant dog's ears,
And roots vibrate as an early warning radar,
But still no smell, no scent,
A rose that does not smell, it is not worthy of the name.

Orang Utang Dear Friend

Oh Orang! Oh Utang!
I came from far to meet and greet you,
The man of old jungle, the name reveals you,
A cute creature human-like denotes,
Through gestures, funny looks
And innocent waving that make you laugh,
If you know how to approach and pat him,
You will be rewarded a touch and may be,
A cuddle,
At your own risk,
A surprise kiss could come like a zephyr,
Octopus-like glue!

Oh Giraffe

Long necked babe and able,
A slippery tongue creature fable,
She enjoyed when being fed,
And does not distinguish blue from red,
Just swallows, eats, and licks the hand,
Like a closer buddy friend,
If you have food in a bag and hand,
They all come in sequence bow and bend,
To grasp their share,
They like to freely borrow but not to lend,
A closer look at them,
And when they get what they want in the end,
They disappear without fear,
How selfish of them my friend!

Snake The Mighty

Snake has been created to deter,
A symbol of power, sex and fear,
Equated with Satan Lucifer and demons in rear,
History where, millions of species,
To speak about listen and hear,
They are Pythons longer enough to devour,
An entire human and swallow him and more,
Anacondas that make your body shiver,
And plenty of fairy and fact stories and lore,
To inform your kind and enrich your folklore,
Adders, vipers and spitting cobras,
That all leave you awake,
Able to cause you death and blindness fainting and ache,
The secret of creation which the Lord could make,
And other species that camouflage themselves and fake,
You in deep jungles, rivers and forests and the alike!

Talking To The Lion Cubs

The Lion they said is a King,
Where kings can only reign and rest,
The lion is a fighter in a ring,
Where all opponents hide in nests,
No one can reveal his name or face,
No one can challenge and take a race,
But baby cubs are approachable,
If you only know how to approach,
And cuter when caressed, adorable,
When lying back rolling and rest!

I Am A Man Of All Seasons

I am a man with a reason
I am a man with life experience and lore,
I am a man of all seasons
Woman! What do you want more?

I am a man with a motto
Neither gambles, nor takes lotto
I am straight
I am right
I am the one who can fight
For his clan and family tribe
And much more
Woman! What do you need me for?
I can be a loving husband,
And a trustworthy friend
If you wish to extend
Your love, trust and the precised core
Of this bond, and be fond of me
Or leave me to elsewhere explore!

The Dance Of Love

Dance of Love,
And dance of passion,
The former is a tradition,
But the latter is a fashion.

Dance of cast,
And dance of must,
When both lack feelings,
All lead to lust!

Dance of business,
And dance of real,
The former is money,
And the latter is a fiddle!

Dance of Tango,
And dance of mango,
The former is love,
And the latter is bango!

What's Love

Love is friendship, respect and desire,
Love, is a bond, trust, warmer than a fire,
Love is a refuge, a shelter and more than what you admire,
In feelings, passion, emotions,
And if it stands firm,
It will surely be stronger than an empire!

Wherever I stand It Will Be My Holy Land

Wherever I stand,
It will be my holy land!
Wherever I stand,
It will be my holy land,
Listen to what I say,
And read my lips Friend!
The world has dramatically changed,
And became difficult to re-fix or amend!
The world of double B, Bush and Blair,
The just, the right became wrong and unfair,
But who would question it now or care?
This reminds of the first boar,
Their entire war machine,
And camel's **** and sand,
For what?

For a Bedouin, who can neither read?
Nor understand,
The ethos of civilised manners,
Of what was once the Arabian nights' land?
Now, if you are referring to tyranny,
I can feed you with a torrent of tyrants,
In the age of globalised plenty,
These are many here and there starting from you,
From where it all began,
From where you are now dictating and
From where you right now stand!
Uncle Sam made a partnership pact with Arabian Sheikhs,
And suddenly these unholy duos call each other ally and friend!

If you are after a might destruction,
Here you have Iraq, Libya,
And now Syria and Yemen,
Difficult to re-fix, or to amend,
And Afghanistan long before them,
Suffered, fell down to its knees and
Sunk into the bloody sand!
My brothers are not biological anymore,
My brothers are not genuine like before,

My true brothers are now those who stand
By me, firm and denounce, protest,
And shout hands in hand!
For peace, justice solidarity that may blend,
Into one world motto and convey the message
The mighty message, to the tribesmen,
The villager, the perceived enemy
And the friend!

Feast In The Middle East

Plow-land vulnerable for plunder,
Source of sins,
I am your victim; i am a pluries, Plunger,
What an onus!
Put on my soft shoulders,
They forced me to side with one of my offspring,
But I refused,
Who would stop the double B, Bush and Blair muster?
Partaking the cake and leaving the debris behind,
For the Chalabis and cos,
My enemies-brothers are now rushing faster,
To dig in my grave before my fate's time,
In a monomania-like manner and attitude,
I am a Persona Extranea,
But Grata, as it is confirmed on this parchment,
My signature, Duplicata.

The highway robbers are set now to move in,
With the blessing of my brothers enemies,
And their masters,
To celebrate the death of a dictator,
And the birth of another one,
For sure, Uncle Sam is not a Mesopotamian,
But now he has a say to lecture on Gilgamesh and his glories,
He is even allowed to guide risk tours around,
What was left of the old saved past?
If not looted or destroyed!
But all what I can say,

Thanks to the torrents of these multi-coloured doves,
Waiting for them with flying, blazing flags,
And slogans of tormented peace,
What a freedom! What a Peace!?
An orchestrated feast in the Middle East...

Rohypnol

They call it Rohypnol,
It keeps your body static,
But snatches your soul,
You're dead but alive,
Sleepy but awake,
Is it real or a fake?
You don't know,
Until you're awake
And find that,
You have been taken
At stake,
Eaten away a la carte as a steak,

Rohypnol, Rohypnol,
Used to hypnotise body and soul,
The younger feels a frail,
Shaky then lead to a fall
It aims at beauty victims
At fresh spring lambs,
With a look and a fashion
With a hook, and a hill,
That ceases instantly,
To feel,

And begins
To faint and kneel
Rohypnol, Rohypnol,
It has an impact and a role
Beware and careful of
What you sip,
And drink and what you dip,
Do not be foolish and don't be fool!
They call it Rohypnol

Read My Reflection

I am not a photogenic,
If you see my word,
You see me,
This is my reflection,
I am what my word says,
I am what my word is,
This is my soul,
I am what my word's power mean!

Beauty From The Orient

When I see your eyes,
I read one hundred and one Arabian nights,
When I see you, I see the shadow of Baghdadi genies,
I see the magical floating carpets...
Flying the sandy dune-like divine bullets,
Racing with stars and more...
Your light, your radiant sparkling eyes paralleled,
With Aladdin's lamps and more,
Your light took the side with the ones in the sky,
With the comet and co, just when i see you,
When i see your hips and swing walk,
Tasting your deeps,
And caressing you and your Garden of Eden,

You're forbidden apples, mango-like,
Touching with style,
Your strawberry lips,
Your olive eyes,
Your Carobian, frizzy hair,
Your longer neck...
And kissing with tenderness,
Your crystal clear-like poll,
I must admit,
And confess to the living world and planet,
That your beauty and look worth keeping,
In esoteric lore-book,
Forever and more.

A Loss Of A Persona

If you shine a shoe you get a tip,
If you brush it well,
You get even a bigger tip,
If you denounce yourself,
And renounce your roots,
You get a reward...you get a nip,
Of the welfare and the system that keep,
Watching you and your progress in deep,
That you may one day cause a serious rip,
And betray your donor and give him a hip,.
Well done keep on brushing...and dig into the deep,
You are not the only one who sweats beyond the break.,
Who sweats beyond the bleep,
They're certainly enough of you...
Very many...on support and on the drip,

It serves you right to suffer since you left your nest,
When you looked down on the mighty debris and the crest,
Of your beloved homeland that was the best,
Now be a living dead with a never-ending rest,
The way you look...the way you talk,
The way you walk and the way you are wrongly dressed,

Your land certainly keeps your head above and pride,
Your land keeps even quieter on your offences and hide,
Your land is still faithful to you..Generous and kind,
If you round the world...reach the skies you won't find,
So generous than her...so merciful...so brave it was signed,
By one million and a half million martyrs,
But today look at yourself...don't play the blind,
Look at your face,
Look at your pace,
Look at all of you...which you won't find,
I think that all of you that was...had certainly died.

Your Teddy Bear's Creed Will Prevail

Your Teddy bear's call will prevail,
No matter how many times it fails,
One million attempts of peace treaties,
But you're still keeping on and on,
Just go...Joy go,
And show the world that you're still brave,
And firm,
I've just started learning from you,
Your creed and perm,
How to confront artificial storms,
And how to prevent armoured vehicles from passing,
With your soft fluffy chest,
And your bear's,
I've just started memorising your peaceful wording song,
And creed,
No fear,
No tear,
No cry,
No agony,
No torments,
Only a simple smile oh! Boy..
No dark,
No bark,
No marks,
On your innocent baby face
Only a red attracting lipsy decoy,
No face,
No pace,
No place for an aggressive spirit,
Only this little bear,
This lovely toy,

Your teddy bear will prevail,
No matter how many times it fails,
No matter how long it takes,
No matter how treacherous,
This worldly life fakes.
I will help you,
I will fix you,

I will do the impossible,
For you and your cute bear,
To enjoy,
A minute of peace will suffice for him and you,
Even a second of this will be enough for both of you,
To dance and shout under the rain,
To dance and swing your fractured hips,
And challenge the artificial rainbow and bullets,
Shout with me and do care,

Shout with me and be fair with your bear,
And yourself,
No more war,
No more bore,
No fighting,
Only a peaceful soul enlightening,
Searching and seeking happiness,
To employ,
This philosophy of Peace,
This philosophy that we are still waiting,
And struggling for.

Love Is Never Blind

Did you test it? Did you find?
Who said that love is blind??
It sees like an eagle into hearts,
The feelings, the blink, the emotions,
It reads the mind,
Love is never blind.

It moves mountains when a need be,
It provokes waves,
It travels into the future,
It takes lives, souls too,
And it generously, gives and gives,
It is kind,
Who said that love is blind?
It quickens and fastens rainy seasons,
It expands spring and summer,
Like twins,
It stretches,
It matches, the sad, sorrow, and,
Joy altogether...It finds,
Who said love is blind??
It is a notion,
Full of emotions,
That all require,
A big desire,
And a will,
A burning fire...
Who said that love is blind,
Is an imposter and a liar...
Love is a beauty,
You seek you'll find,
Love is always there,
Waiting to strike its arrows,
With the Cupid angel,
Whom we all know,
At hearts...
Like darts...
It never misses,
Its target...With a flaming word...

With a red rose...
With a kiss...
With a hug...
With a clumsy jump,
With a funny look,
 With a nervous breakdown,

With fear[s],
With tears,
But never blind...if you do care and mind,
Love is never blind...

Is it easy for the one who leaves?
Or for the one who stays alone, behind?
Please tell me, because I could neither answer,
Nor could I find.

They told me that who leaves,
Cries for a so beloved place,
And gets used to a soul,
Which he began to cherish and face,

But the one who stays behind,
Cries of loneliness,
And for a left loved one,
Then becomes a hermit in holiness,

Both of them suffer a broken heart,
Heads over heals lovably blind,
Both them have their causes,
Their will and readiness,
To justify their deeds and action,
With love and pure affection.
It was prescribed that love is never blind,
But coincidence and fate create its environment,
In the end, love is never blind!

No Blame On You Woman

No blame on you..
No blame on you woman,
To stand and yell,
No blame on you lady,
To shout and fight!!
No blame on you,
To lose your reason,
To miss your season,
To lose control, temper and sight.
When your pride has gone with dust,
Approached and left as source of lust,
By....men sons of men,
Fountain of promises, Streams of lies,
Arrogance and disgust!
Will you still believe and put your trust?
On the sexist..Retrograde..
On the still.. A maniac pat!
Is it wrong or is it right??
To become a sex symbol..?
A commodity..?
To please the Pratt?

You lost your status...You lost your pride...
Your virginity,
And you did not mind,
You lost your femininity,
Your Victorian teachings,
You escaped the past,
And here you're today fighting the present,
Your cause is a "Must",
Nobody cares...Except you...
Only you...You! Are by God,
An immortal...
A respected wife,
A cherished sister...
A sweet daughter,
A beloved mother...Here you last!

Shopoholic

Shop...Shop till you'll drop,
And enjoy life more..And hope,
Remember that you only live today,
But tomorrow you may not be able to cope,
With the hardship, with the life style,
Remember, that life is a string,
With a fragile ring,
And a loose rope,

Shop...Shop...till you'll drop,
Since you have the money,
The sweet honey,
Why not then..Pop'
In all the stores,
Scan all the floors,
And throw your sop,
To the shop-keeper,
The money nipper,
Let him...mop!

Shop... don't think how it goes,
God only...knows,
Just shop until you get tired and drop,
Pierre Cardin,
Laura Ashley...Armani,
Channel...top woman and man top,
Don't waste time,
Melt with grandeur and fame,
Taste everything..Sweet and sour,
Buy anything... and for the priceless hope,
Walk and run,
Right...left and have fun,
But avoid the killing dope.

The Witch Party

Whoever sees me,
Fancies me,
And fancies my look,
Body and my entire,
Whoever touches me,
Loves me...
And who loves me,
Gets attracted to my desire,
Whoever approaches me,
Wants me, and wants more, my exotic warmth,
And my burning fire,
Whoever talks to me,
Gets charmed,
By my tender voice,
And becomes my living slave,
Subjected to my empire,
I'm the powerful, I'm the one,
I'm the wonderful, I'm who can,
Right the wrong,
Transform a human into a frog,
Charm the good, and make the evil,
Change the mood, entertain the Devil,
You better submit to my will,
And listen to what I say,
You're alive-dead who does not feel,
If I may,
Add that your soul is already mine,
It is a sign,
That you're a freak,
Feasibly weak,
And do exactly what I tell,
You...you are in Hell,
You and I,
Signed a contract,
You and he signed the mighty tract,

With a drop of blood...of yours,
The seals, the names that all endorse,
Your confirmation,

Your invitation,
To Lucifer,
And his fellows,
Arepo and Rotas,
The occult secret,
You're now part of the Sabbath feast,
Now be ready to copulate with the beast,
You're now a newborn omen,
You're a heretic...you're his host,
And if you don't repent your deeds,
You're surely lost.

Mongol phobia And The Eastern Horde

Neither a fable,
Nor a tale,
This is a fact,
A story to tell,
To everyone, female and male.
To generations, younger and frail.

About a threat, a monster from the East,
That struck the world like a beast,
Attacked Europe by cold and mist,
Oceans of horsemen, millions at least,
Ravaged cathedrals, and crucified the priest,

How to cope and fight and face the ghoul?
How to reason with a barbarian, a crazy fool?
How to prevent a suicidal conflict to pacify and cool?
How to save the lore, the patrimony and the living soul?
How to reconcile with the unknown and use the best tool?
That was the question...
That was the wisdom to lead and rule,

The Pope decided to answer in peace,
Then sent Carpini after a blessing..And a kiss,
Advising him to inform...and not to miss,
To meet the Eastern father, son nephew and niece,
To call for salvation and the Chris,

As soon as the monk began to trace,
With a great shock he started to face,
An unusual nation that was in race,
With time, with weather, with the cosmos and space,
No one could classify it, No one could place,
Its barbarity, Nay! Its grace,

They consume everything, greens, pulses including rice,
They are carnivorous, they eat mice,
They spare not a single creature, including lice,
All seem to them, healthy and nice,
They worship Shamanism, horses and they play dice,

They conquer for pleasure, and race with the skies,
When Çarpini reached the rising sun,
The great Mongol..The supreme Khan,
Who crashed Empires, who enslaved the Han,
Who scared newborn babies, woman and man,
Who, no one refused him, and who dared had to run,
For his life, for his family, for his entire clan,
Then Carpini approached the formal bar,
And addressed himself to the Lord Tatar,
Explaining to him that he came from far,
To preach Christendom not the Latin Lar,

Before the monk finishing his say,
The lord stood up! Angrily, with a reply,
"Go back to your Pope! Before I'll flay,
You" and tell him that the Tatar ray,
Is invincible in a warfare-play,

Fearful, the priest returned deceived,
More than what he saw and what he perceived,
How would he break the news? How would he read?
The powerful message, the humiliating creed!
In the end, he stood on his heart and then he did,

Europe was ready for the Great War,
Nations of the crucifix, thousands and more,
The bells of alarm sounded the lands, and the shore,
To prevent the conquest, that was the heart! And the core!
The calls were "fight or flight" or seal your door!

But halfway...they turned blind,
To change plan, they did not mind,
To strike east, and there to find,
A city of lore of rich and kind,
Baghdad the marvel that enlightens the blind,

There! They killed; they mutilated in countless,
There! They burnt libraries that were priceless!
They pillaged, they raped they were heartless,
No mercy, no help, the Baghdadis were helpless,
To defend themselves against the infidel
Barbarian Godless!
No place was spared from vandalism,

Places of worship and mysticism,
Circles of learning and sciolism,
Poetry, literature and euphemism,
All had gone with "Gog and Magog" the cataclysm!
But "Ain Jalout" was the battlefield,
For generations to pick and read,
In history, and faith and heretical creed,
Where all religions had met indeed,

In a bloody war, all had to bleed,
In the end, the Armageddon had to finish,
To slow the spiting dragon and diminish,
Its arrogance, its myth and tarnish,
Its long lasting reputation, had to vanish,
Forever to allow another war and a skirmish.
How would I judge? What would I say?

Was it a truth or was it a lie?
Genghis Khan, and Kublai Khan,
Hulaku, Munghe Khan and low and high,
Were they all barbarians, or were all lasting heroes not to die?
This is the last verse and point to specify.

I Want To Be With You

I want to be with you,
I want to be what you want me to,
But I only wish to be what you want me,
I have lost my name,
My persona and I am now, only for you,
if you only wish me to be with you,
But promise that you will be for me,
When it rains and be my refuge,
Because if you do, I will always be with you,
If you want me to,
I just want to be with you

Be Realistic

Every beautiful story has got an end,
This is the logic to accept my friend,
No matter how you challenge it,
No matter how you build barriers,
Cut bridges,
You won't be able to neither prevent,
Nor fix it, or amend,

Every sea has a limit and a shore,
Every boundary has a natural fence,
A gate, or a door,
But what would remain my dear,
Is to face a bitter reality and to wish for,
The good the bad and sour sweet memories of the past,
That may enhance or reduce your sadness,
Or take you back to your senses like before.

Aroma-Poetry

Mother nature oh! Rose of roses!
Mother of all flowers' and smell,
Ylang Ylang! You don't know what it causes!
An aphrodisiac turns you on like hell!

Sandalwood with its masculine warmth poses,
Rosemary clears the head, you can tell,
Peppermint purifies blocked noses,
Patchouli the meditative, it does sell,

Orange oil refreshing, stimulates since Moses,
Chamomiles in variety and bluebell,
Mandarin the sweet floral in few doses,
Helps you digest and makes feeling very well,

Marjoram helps a positive mood,
In creating and lemon oil reduces the stress,
Lavender the cleansing oil is surely good,
Juniper Berry soothes and tones the muscles in mess,

Geranium the relaxing prepares you for action,
Cypress oil relaxes you twice and once again,
Cedarwood calms and makes ready for attraction,
Basil oil with prairie's odours is the main,

With Myrtle the antiseptic and carminative,
And Niaouli the beverage that it was,
For Neroli, the aphrodisiac is very active,
Origanum, Pimento, Pine oil and Rose,

Pettigrain, this is a citrus vulgaris,
Calms anger and refreshes the mind,
And the sedative, hypotensive Amyris,
With Angelica the stimulation you will find,

The Aniseed, Pimpinella anisum,
An antiemetic, diuretic and an insecticide,
Likewise in Anise-star, illicium verum,
All the same remedies you will find,
Laurus Nobilis, this is Bay-leaf oil,

Analgesic, cholagogue and hepatic,
In sweet styrax, Benzoin when you boil,
Vanilla flavour, a deodorant and cephalic,

Citrus Bergamia, Bergamot like orange,
An uplifting in character for anxiety,
In Birch tar, Betula Lenta you need courage,
To kill pain and thank the Lord Almighty,

Black Pepper, piper nigrum spicy sharp,
Cajuput oil, the herbaceous and penetrating,
In a singing-like circle with a harp,
Helps the heart, and respiration in circulating,

Cinnamomum Camphora that's Camphor,
Since Chrosroes the Babylonian King the wise,
Surely was part of civilisation and folklore,
For the Eastern powers that fall and rise!

Caraway, Carum Carvi is sweet!
And a flavouring agent in all your food,
Adding it when marinating your meat,
Aromatise the entire dish that will be good!

Cardamom, Elettaria yellow flower and pale,
Very spicy and digestive from the East,
The Arabs praise it in their coffee call it "Hail",
And the Romans took it after each great feast,

Carrot-seed, Daucus carota has a past,
In skin diseases, teeth and gums and the sight illness,
Its effect on red blood cells is very fast,
With the right blends it surely helps the body fitness,

Apium Graveolens, celery is fresh and warm,
That was a symbol of funerals, death and grief,
It was believed in ancient Egypt nay in Rome,
To cure swollen limbs and to relieve,

Cymbopogon Nardus that's Citronella,
In wax candles helps mosquitoes to disappear,
Its oil is used to beautify and make the "Bella",
In look and smell and feeling...what's more to hear??

Clove, coriander and clary Sage,
Cumin, Elemi and Dill,
Thousands of oils won't fill the page,
Eucalyptus and Fennel they heal,

Fir, Frankincense and Galbanum,
Garlic, Ginger and Grapefruit,
Guaicwood, Hyssop and Helichrysum,
This is immortelle oil to suit,

Jasminum, the waiting King at the doors,
A perfume for lovers to indicate,
A seduction imported by the moors,
To Spain, then Europe to fabricate,

Its uses along with Lavandin,
This hybrid of true Lavender and spike,
Was exploited in soap trade to begin,
Then turned to perfume-making and the alike,

Lemongrass is a very reviving,
And Lime, this citrus medica,
It does match when mixed with Mandarin,
And with Nutmeg could be a "replica,"

Linden Blossom oil is a slightly spicy,
Litsea Cubeba is a floral and fruity,
In Melissa, the honey-bee you fancy,
And Myrrh the musky, symbol for beauty,

Palmarosa, they say "clarifies the mind,
And Parsley was named after "Petros,
In Pine oil, good feelings you will find,
Rosemary has affected "Ethos",

Rosewood, this "Bois de rose",
A "Jacaranda" is known in Brazil,
A real deodorant in dose!
Sage was believed in Rome "To heal,"
Pimento is known as "Allspice,
And Santolina is still a pillar in medicine,
With Spearmint the smell is very nice,
In Tagetes the citrus flavour is never lasting,

Tangerine the hypnotic and Tarragon,
Terebinth the balsamic the vermifuge,
Thyme the thymus vulgaris that was born,
From the tears of Helen-Troy that grew huge,

Tea-Tree oil is sanitary Australian,
Verbena makes a love potion pot-pourri,
Vetivert, this earthy fragrance's never alien,
To the world of perfumes, competition and fury,

On Violet the odorata was said,
A symbol of fertility in Greece,
The perfume that Marie Antoinette preferred,
And in Yarrow a help for diabetes.

Baby TV

I knew Uganda through Aids,
I knew India through a flood,
I knew Cambodia through raids,
I knew Bangladesh through mud,

I knew Ethiopia through starvation,
And the Sudan fundamental horror,
South Africa...not to mention,
And the Arab only through terror,

Now I'm a real well informed,
A real cultured gentleman,
I can stand for a mastermind contest,
And I will definitely win it
Glory to the mighty Baby TV,
Peace be upon the Baby,
The one who can neither hear,
Nor see,
But knows more than Madame Soleil,
Who pretends to predict the future..And foresee

A Southern Voice From A Northern City

A Southern voice,
From a Northern city,
Life is harsh,
There is no pity
You beg
You crawl...
You cry your way out...
No one would come to your safety,
No one would dare,
It is all grey selfish...and blur
No shoulder to lean on..
To tell your story and mourn,
It is all a cruel world,
It is all...an enmity.
You're alone,
But not on your own,
Thousands like you are calling,
There are thousands like you who are struggling,
In this worldly life,
In this double-faced doll,
Good and evil, Ugly and pretty.

On Your Birthday

Twenty-six springs came soon,
To throne the shiny sun,
Susan H...The smiling moon,
To the stars that rushed and ran,
To surround this splitting "Lune",
To share happiness and fun,

On this planet shape in Dune,
A blooming rose came to light,
Greeting the lilies and prune,
Sparkling stars had to fight,
Which one would be close to June?

To May, April and March the bright,
To bow and sing and play in tune,
And make echoes from a stalactite,
None of them is really immune,
They all praise your name and sight

They all came in twenty-six,
They all came to book and fix,
For this lovely month to learn,
To light your candles and burn,
An angelic incense to celebrate
Susan! To celebrate your day,
Joy grandeur might!

Mother-Nature

Mother Nature...Oh! Blue water,
Oh! Soft Globe...
I'm your slave; I'm your probe,
I'm for you... and for what you hold,
I'm a nature addict, this what I was told,
I like your fresh air...I like your breeze,
I like your flowery plants,
I like your shading trees,
I like all your little creatures....
Squirrels, wild rabbits, birds and bees,

I like the odours of your virgin prairies and farms,
I like the magical beauty of your countryside that charms,
Hunters, adventurers and lovers more...
Vagabonds and even fugitives who come for,
Seeking shelters to escape and hide,
Horses-lovers and jockeys who ride,
I like your singing rivers that show and lean,
I like your floating swans going in twin [s],
I like the tiny alleyways that lead and mean,
Paths, short cuts, mews...all in green,

I like your braying donkeys and the barking dog,
I like the whistling winds and your splashy bog,
I like your orphan turtles and the leaping frog,
I like your frosty mornings and your ghostly fog,
I like your stylish gardens...I like your vogue,
I like everything in you, mother-nature,
But I don't deserve you...
Since I'm destroying you,
And myself [...] I'm a rogue!!

Nostalgia

I just came to see,
What was left, but there was nothing for me…to enjoy,
But the only cry of the old, nostalgic memories,
And bless once upon a time my dear companions,
Dead? Migrated? Rebelled? Flipped or changed town,
Hence after a while, I decided to return back, to see and remember,
I came with the spirit of the drums,
Full of energy and hotness of the beloved continent,
I came with an open heart and arms,
To hug and kiss the remained debris and sweet memories,

I came to clean the dusty, humble sitting spots,
Where I used to rest and cross my legs and narrate
Some weird, fairy tales to the small little men,
Lads token of my beloved old estate...
I came back to see and wished never came to see what I saw,
Just to live the old beautiful stories and memories.

You Are My Rainbow

You are my rainbow when nature needs one,
You are my rainy season when the fields get thirsty,
You are my whole when I need to have fun,
With you to make me feel back to my twenty,
You are my radiant light,
My sunny arrows by day and night,
And my comet,
Sparkling by night,
You are my ship,
You are my dip,
You are my entire journey,
You are my flight!

The Wall Has Got Eyes And Ears

Who speaks does indeed lie,
Who does not, surely knows more,
But keeps silent by fear to die,

The Walls have ears,
To listen and hear,
The brother became a foe to testify,
A brother sells a brother,
In this deep, dark room,
Under the torch blow!
Body parts here and there, exposed,
To the naked eye!

In the X room,
In between the butler's hands,
The truth and evidence are baklava-like
Fabricated and made,
In that sweep clean sink,
God has been mentioned one million and a half times,
But no hear…no see!
The law of Amorta is above all laws,

My witnesses are solid static objects to say,
A bottle, a spanner, a screwdriver,
A hammer and an electric tool to go,
To accomplish the job,
The dirty job, you've guessed what next to do!

Bastards have adopted names and,
Became respected men,
Old grannies are raped in turn and in presence of their beloved ones,
Old grannies turned delightful virgins, and were re-raped again,
Simple mothers who backed the first November bread were sliced,
Like mad!!
Dogs ceased to bark like before,
Cats became sheepish and were all kept indoors,
Their presence also ceased to scare rats and mice,
Along the streets, boulevards and corridors,

And morality, honour, pride and co,
Were all sold in the black market,
For a cheap Dinar and in that store,
Or were all buried in the sand,
Or were all soaked with this mighty black gold,
Or were all lit with a match to blow, blow…blow!

Scared to death where death becomes now only a nirvana,
Scared as a shaking leaf,
Scared not to die, but scared to witness and testify,
Your own soul is coming out of you,
Out of your being in a slow motion,
Whilst you are still bleaking,
Not a single scream, nor a single cry!

You plead guilty or not,
No one can protect you,
Or shade,
Nessuno comes to your salvation, Mai,
No one comes to your salvation,
Whether you tell the whole truth, or a fabricated lie!
Hooligans and outlaws were forced to march in uniform,
And were called the sons of nation,
To help, to save a war of gains and privatisation,

Kids if not slaughtered or kidnapped,
Are given sweets and short religious sermons,
On patriotism and are used to decorate road-sides,
And put on stage to boost a song and a play...
Hey…hey…hey….!

But bastards remain always bastards,
By God almighty! Earth and sky!
The filthy flesh remains always stinky,
Even if camouflaged with a fragrant scented high,
And in what a true perfume could mean and signify!

Saro Cui Inshallah

Saro inshallah cui!
Saro encora cui con un millione
Dei vocaboli sul la pace,
Sull'amore,
La fraternita e tutto,
Con un branch of olives and a howling message which you already all know,
A reminder, please remember my voice,
If I disappear, just remember the tone and you will recognise me,
You will recognise my message,
Just peace be upon thee and all of you.
I have the right to live like any other creatures on this space,
The right like any living soul occupying this place,
To vivere la tranquilita, la pace and the pride,
Please quote me whenever you feel like writing,
Quote me wherever you go,
I am a human, a being who wishes to be,
Simple, lives, breathes and contributes.
Thank you…

Just For You And Your Eyes Only

You are sweet, charming and delight,
For your eyes only,
For your entire you,
I stand firm and fight,
Your feminine look, body is slender,
Your firmness, your waist,
Your listeners are all wrong,
But you, you are always right,
What can I say?
Everything is good,
And beyond description in you,
About you,
You all,
Together as whole,
You are the creation of the might!

Lovely Sara

I've heard the moon whispering to the stars
About your beauty about your olive eyes
One lost its way,
One fells in you universe,
But another still fading away,
Here it dies.
They all swore that no one would shine again,
No one would rise!
Since your radiant face shining in size.

They all swore to remain in hiding and be disguised,
Since you're still shining on them,
They're all amazed.
I've heard the springy waters singing your name
Praising your beauty, praising your fame,
The lyrics were simple repeating the same,
Oh lovely Sara! In look and name
I've seen the nightingale singing in cage,
I've seen the parrot in wild in rage,
Picking minty leaves and sage,
Shouting and shouting without blame.
I've seen the sun setting down in shyness,
For your undeclared title your highness,
You're a princess of joy, smile, and finesse,
You babysit the elder, the young and the baby-boy.
Your innocent look your childish nose,
Your ringy mouth, your chicks in rose,
Your strawberry lips your tongue in pose,
They all in place like a pretty toy.
Your tar oiled hair,
Your skin is fair,
My sight is blurring,
I've lost it boy!
Your thighs and lips,
Your kiss and tips,
Your bosom and hips,
Are you an attraction or a divine decoy??
Your scruffy hair is a blossomed flower,
Showing its petals higher and lower,
Indicating directions like a tower.

The Year Of Sour Sweet Africa

The mask has been dropped,
The black tar has faded away,
The red muddy potatoes have been cleaned.
The land has turned green,
The dead body has been washed away,
The ghosts of river Victoria have brought their fays,
The racism,
The therapy,
Are all over under way,
Hey! Hey! Hey!

The sky became blue again,
The migrant sparrow came back to the motherland,
The Steve Biko's spirit shaded the crowd,
Ahmed Savana' called like mad,
The Amanda,..
The little orphans found adopting parents,
The widow, the widower, the homeless came to dine,
Life is fine,
Life is all now joy,
Under the ANC boy,
The black...is back,
Mandela is here,
After a decade, after a Bogota,
After a tyranny, and after a Declerck!

Refugitive

I am the migrant soul,
I am the fugitive from fear,
I am the scapegoat tool,
I am who made life dear,

I am what they want me to be,
I am a fugitive...And a refugee.

I am an alien...an intruder from space,
I have no status..Nor rights or place,
Whatever I do I'll be the same,
Whatever I say I'll have the blame,
What a disgrace! And what a shame!

I told them that I have only one face,
I play fair, compete and race,
I even pay taxes..I keep the country tidy like they do,
I walk straight and tighten my lace,
That no one could slip on and creates a case,
To make my life hell...to make me lose face,

But they still decide to keep the name,
To act in double and remain the same,
What a disgrace! And...What a shame

A Beauty From The Garden Of Eden

Whenever the rays of the sun begin to fade,
And the twilight hours and dawn appear,
Whenever the stars begin rushing to queue and ride,
Their skylights' ships tearing the zephyr,
Your radiant beauty emerges to cover and shade,
All this universe, front, middle and rear,
How can I describe it? How is it made?
Only God almighty knows it well my dear,
Your spring smile overcomes winter and fastens the year,
But when you're sad bursting into tears,
It calls winter again, flashing its lightening and thundering its blade,
This is only a small verse and a mere,
Description of your emerald dew,
Flooding diamonds over your chicks are laid,
I could neither torment myself to go further or hear,
My eyes are full of lights, your light and shade!

To Diana The Queen Of Hearts

Princess of love,
A queen of hearts,
By your departure,
By your flight,
You tore the nation,
In pieces and parts,
I lost the words, nor could I borrow,
To describe the pain, sadness and sorrow,
Of a nation in mourning,
That woke up by morning,
To find a Queeny, departing earlier than tomorrow,
By your departure,
By your plight,
To the skies,
To mighty mite,

The world is sad,
The mood is bad,
The young is mad,
Of agony and more sorrows,
The fate is fate,
No one can date,
Nor predict, the destiny,
Today or tomorrow,
Younger in her prime,
Younger golden time,
Found her rightly prince,
Her ultimate Dodi her beloved hero,
But suddenly, departed with him and co,
What a loss! What a grief! And what a sorrow!
In the baby thought,
Her goodness and action,
In the poor and the needy's,
Her complete affection,

She was the icon,
She was the beacon,
She was the model,
In her complexion,

The fields will remember,
The fields will retain,
The dark August and September,
The tragedy and main,
News and queues!
And deposed roses,
By gates and mews!
A baby crying poses,
Everyone will mourn,
Everyone will weep,
The coffin, in morning, and at down,
Neither words to add nor to borrow,
To describe the sadness and sorrow.

I Offer U An Onion

I offer you an onion,
Instead of an apple,
That's all what I can offer you,
For the time being,
I can tell you now,
And reveal what's in the parcel,
Do not get excited, do not expect,

I don't want you to have the shock and the effect,
Do not get moved by the red-shiny ribbon,
It is not a branded one,
It is my work, my humble creation,
It is my art if you say so,
It is my imagination,
It is the thought...The sign which counts,
They say...

You knew well that I was what I'm...
I'm an empty garden that can grow,
Only modest things,
Basic things, Poor things,
I don't know when and where,
I get my beloved one, a rosy apple,
The life apple as they say,
I wonder when and when my star will shine again,
And enlightens the fields,
And brings back the smile, the joy and the fun,
That once was,

I still remember,
I still recall,
The lilies, the blue-bells,
The mimosas, the chamomiles..
The lemon...the apple-trees and all,
The various fruits in abundance,
But all that was the past,
Gone with dust,
Please be patient,
And ask your heart to wait,

For the next promising spring,
May be it will be my destiny and fate,
To get you more than an apple,
As my beloved wishes,
Or maybe it will be very late,
For me, for you, or for us both to topple,

This poverty-mine monotony system!
But for the time being,
Accept this humble dried onion,
I'm a barren field,
That produces only rocks,
 And nothing else.

To Susan On Valentines

I don't believe in St. Valentine,
Nor in the sanctity of this day,
But all I wish that you would be mine,
With...or without a folkloric Fay!

Accept this bunch...this rose retain,
As a token and a souvenir!
May I hope that we will remain
Closer and more in the future near.

I do respect the other creed,
Customs and norms that you follow,
And also those who praise indeed,
The lord almighty and hallow,

His name and throne and holy bid!
His sacred books that turned sallow,
From them his messengers decreed,
The teachings that we all wallow,
With an open mind oh! Please accept,
This verse and message from my heart,
Feelings which none can intercept,
Or break them even if he is smart!

Break-Up

Take your rose and don't come back again,
Just go,
We are not for each other anymore,
Although,
We met,
We met, friendly by chance,
And here we are now...enemies,
Here we are...worse than rivals...
Here we're now...Pitiless foe(s),
I don't believe in dreams,
Nor in a made-up stories,
Nor in crocodiles' tears,
Like they do,
All is a fake...
All is a lie,
All is - for me - a corrupted law.

The New Disorder

We were the children of the revolution,
We're the last of the past struggle,
We are the children of the evolution,
We are the day of fun, joy and emotion.
We cried the dark colonial disaster,
We're still crying blaming the master,
We're left behind quickly and faster,
How could it be; what the notion??
Oh! Brother, tell me what's the solution?
Oh! Brother show me how to be cautioned,
Should I regain the bush and kill the Bush,
Or should I melt into the fusion?
It's on its way they call it "order",
Making its day through disorder,
Crashing Empires, breaking the border[s],
They call it freedom without caution.
No king; no Prince, no spared Khan,
From the "Baltics" to all "Kistans",
Sooner or later it'll reach the "Han",
Is it right or an intrusion?
How could you then brandish your gun?
At "Patriot" you son of a Hun,
When millions of bombs coming in tons,
Engrave a city
Without pity
Killing the masses in a slow motion,
Is it people's will for war?
Is it the masters' call of whore?
All these massacres!...What all this for?
Politics of "Peace" exclusion!
Is it a fact or an illusion?
Just tell me brother with no confusion,
Is it time for peace "revolution"?
This is the problem, this is the core.

One Million And A Half Stories On The Art Of Torture

Nobody moves...nobody talks,
And who dares...gets sharp folks,
Stuff his mouth...stuff her rear,
Terror reigns and tearing fear,

Disfigured being a pierced face,
To whomsoever present my case?
They are all backing his daily deed,
This new species...inhuman breed,

Countless kids they're all slain
Like Abel by Brother Cain,
Ali does not need his bath,
Because he had it already red,

Nor Omar needs to eat,
He had the entire menu and a treat,
Can't you see his swollen tummy,
Wrapped like an Egyptian mummy?

Torture is still on,
Celebrating one million and a half at down,
With a French bleach,
And an Italian stitch,
With a Spanish applause,
And an Anglo-Saxon's pose.

The French Nuclear Spit

The Tahitian sparrows won't sip,
The Albatross won't dive deep,
The pelican, the islander
Poorer than before,
Has to suffer and keep...
The agony...inside him and her,
And the world at large is watching,
The tyranny...
The imperialism that was once before,
Here it comes once again,
To poison your rips,
French foe..Foe,
Three two one go...bang!
Spare me Francois, it is Joe...
Who would suffer...
Go general...just go,
Deep...deep and on the surface blow

Poems Behind The Bars

Poems behind the bar[s],
Begging...calling from high and far,
Oh! God, mighty Akbar,
Whiten our souls from dirt and tar!

Help us to bring back the whiteness to the city,
And sow a climate of love and pity,
Our hearts are rotten with revenge,
And throned with hatred and blind enmity,

Help us to change and transform
The mourning and the yelling that inform,
The screams of victims who roam,
The dark empty corridor(s),

Into a joyful yuyulation,
And a baby-babbling jubilation,
The friendly gossips and fascination,
Of the laborious quarters and more,

To recall the nightingale-like gathering,
The family bond and fathering,
The story-telling of granny-mothering,
The fairy-tails and folklore,

The early prayers and Adhan,
And the break-fasting in peace-Aman,
But now we're living under a ban,
Under the General and his 'military corps.'

One Thousand And One Bombs On Baghdad

We were accustomed to read one thousand
And one night in Baghdad,
Tonight the glorious city-sky is sad,
It sounded bang! Bang
Where is my mummy? Where is my dad?
Are they all alive under the cruise wreckage?
Or are they all dead?

The a 'Rashid city was weeping,
It rained hatred,
It rained prejudiced,
It rained cactus of different shapes,
They're all aliens,
Some were homemade,
They're all colourful,
In blue, in yellow and in red.
Do you still remember brother?
Because if you don't I still do
What the big Satan, Lucifer what he said!

The cross versus the crescent, take it or leave it,
An entire racism by the media was also fed.
Some hidden in a banker,
Others crawling of hunger,
Others demonstrating with anger,
Pale, yellowish faces they all looked bad.
Where is my nation, my Arabity and my Islam?
Oh Mutasamahh! Where are my brothers?
Are they all dead???
They called it precise bombing and it was right indeed,
In the heart of the baby-heart
Like the British game of dart,
The arrow hit its target,
It hit it like mad.
Nobody moves a finger,
In the age of Patriot and Stinger,
They all believe in star-wars, economic prosperity,
They all believe in the Pope, pop-star singer,

They all believe that one-day Allah would side with them to defeat,
The neo-Thamud and Aad,
They're all waiting for the coming future Mahdi,
And for the Armageddon battle to be led.

Love-Roots

I love you before love itself was born,
And the feelings were created and made,
I loved you before Venus sounded her horn,
To appear from the sea and shade,
The Hellenic beauty-virgins who mourn,
The lack of men, who ride,
Sea-horses and chase the mermaid,
And the legends of the unicorn,
And the fairy-tales that were laid,
To the old past the...unworn,

The One Who Loves U

Go after the one, who loves you,
And leave the one you think you love,
The former will surely please you,
And help you to keep your head above,
The latter will simply damp you,
And push you into the unknown to dive
For her satanic wimps and fame,
You crazy fool, she will drive,
You and how many men like you,
Were stuck to get out safer and alive?

Beauty-Doll

I've seen my shadow in your eyes,
I've seen my double in you all,
I've seen it slow how it dies,
Rehearsing like an actor changing role [s],
Your bluebell shiny sight is attractive,
Your spring-like smile is a call,
Your flashy blink is very active,
When animating your beauty...mole,
Your brown hair is really matching,
Your baby-face like a doll,
Your longer neck is also catching,
With your crystal front and the poll.

INDEX